IMAGES
of America

SAN ANTONIO
IN THE GREAT WAR

D1608326

Standing near their cantonment barracks, these new Army recruits are executing present arms while at the position of right shoulder arms. Like the tens of thousands of doughboys who flooded into all of the military installations in the San Antonio area in 1917, they are learning the job of soldiering. (Courtesy of the Fort Sam Houston Museum.)

ON THE COVER: Aviation cadets, identified by the white band on their campaign hats, arrive at Kelly Field, south of downtown San Antonio. They are typical of more than 200,000 doughboys who flowed into the training camps around the Alamo City during the "war to end all wars" for service "over there." (Courtesy of the Air Education and Training Command.)

IMAGES
of America

SAN ANTONIO
IN THE GREAT WAR

John M. Manguso

ARCADIA
PUBLISHING

Published by Arcadia Publishing
Charleston, South Carolina

Printed in the United States of America

Library of Congress Control Number: 2013954267

For all general information, please contact Arcadia Publishing:
Telephone 843-853-2070
Fax 843-853-0044
E-mail sales@arcadiapublishing.com
For customer service and orders:
Toll-Free 1-888-313-2665

Visit us on the Internet at www.arcadiapublishing.com

*To John Riola and all who have had the courage and the wisdom
to participate in the defense of the United States of America*

CONTENTS

Acknowledgments — 6

Introduction — 7

1. "One of the Heavens" — 11

2. San Antonio's Army Post — 29

3. "The Mother of Armies" — 45

4. "Where America's Eagles Hatch" — 61

5. America's Foremost Air Service Flying School — 83

6. "Hell's Fire and Fuzzie-O" — 91

7. "When Johnny Came Marching Home" — 101

8. Where Are They Now? — 115

About Preservation Fort Sam Houston — 127

ACKNOWLEDGMENTS

The majority of the images in this volume appear courtesy of the Fort Sam Houston Museum (FSHM), the historical offices of the Air Education and Training Command (AETC) at Randolph Air Force Base and the US Air Force Personnel Center (US Air Force Photograph), the Library of Congress (LOC), and the Historic American Building Survey (HABS). For their help in providing the images in this book, I thank Martin Callahan of the Fort Sam Houston Museum; Anne K. Hussey and Erin N. Rice at the AETC Historical Office; Rudy Purificato, historian at the US Air Force Personnel Center at Randolph Air Force Base; and Mark Frye at Port San Antonio for their assistance.

I would also like to thank: Ruth Dunmire, my first history teacher, for getting me interested in history; Dr. John K. Mahon, my advisor in graduate school at the University of Florida; Brig. Gen. Joseph P. Kingston, who gave me my job as commander of the Military History Detachment; Maj. Gen. Henry Mohr, chief of the Army Reserve, who advised me to "tell it like it is, even if no one believes you"; Maj. Bennie Boles, who hired me as a museum curator at Fort Sam Houston; Col. Jim O'Neal, Ed Miller, and Ron Still, three of the best supervisors a museum director could have; Joan Gaither, whose support as president of Preservation Fort Sam Houston has been invaluable; Martha Doty Freeman; and Laura Bruns, my editor at Arcadia Publishing, who provided support and guidance throughout the preparation of this book. Special thanks goes to Jacqueline Davis, who has been my strong right arm for most of my 33 years at the Fort Sam Houston Museum. Most of all, I thank my beloved wife of 47 years, Barbara, whose support has been and continues to be . . . priceless.

INTRODUCTION

In August 1914, the assassination of Archduke Franz Ferdinand in Sarajevo plunged Europe into a world war. This war was called the Great War for Civilization, or simply the Great War. The United States would stay out of World War I until April 1917. Nevertheless, things began to happen in and around San Antonio, Texas, which would start the Alamo City on the path to becoming "Military City, USA."

San Antonio has been known as Military City, USA, for many years. By the time the Korean War started, the city had five major military installations: Fort Sam Houston and Kelly, Brooks, Randolph, and Lackland Air Forces Bases. The city has always had a military role, regardless of which flag flew over it. Spain stationed troops here in 1718 to protect the local missions. They were replaced by Mexican troops in 1820. By 1836, the Texians under Gen. Sam Houston expelled the Mexican Army, thereby forming the Republic of Texas. Under the republic, San Antonio was a base for the Texian Army and the Texas Rangers.

Statehood brought the US Army into Texas. In October 1845, while annexation legislation was in progress in Washington, the 2nd Regiment of Dragoons entered San Antonio, becoming its first US Army garrison. The city soon added a quartermaster supply depot and headquarters of the 8th Military District. These activities, along with the small garrison, operated out of rented buildings. There were no Army-owned buildings in the city until 1859, when the San Antonio Arsenal was built. The troops in San Antonio secured the border with Mexico and protected the settlements from hostile Native American depredations. The city soon saw its first mobilization when troops assembled in town under Gen. John E. Wool for operations in northern Mexico during the Mexican-American War. After the war, the headquarters in San Antonio commanded as many as 25 posts with up to a quarter of the entire Army. This set the pattern for the future. Each conflict would result in the accretion of addition troops, facilities, or missions for the Army in San Antonio.

The military facilities in San Antonio were surrendered to secessionist forces in February 1861, but the military missions of San Antonio remained the same. Federal troops returned in 1865, resulting in another change in management. After Reconstruction, operations against hostile tribes occupied the Army in Texas. As these hostilities tapered off, Gen. William Tecumseh Sherman sought to reduce the cost of maintaining garrisons in Texas by reducing the number of posts, which had reached a high of 38 in 1867. General Sherman began closing surplus military posts and concentrating their garrisons in San Antonio. The city's central location and existing military infrastructure made it the logical place to concentrate troops, who could respond to any trouble spot in the region.

To avoid the high cost of renting facilities, the War Department considered moving out of San Antonio. As this would be bad for San Antonio, the city council offered a parcel of land outside of town for a permanent post. The offer was accepted, and construction of a new quartermaster depot was begun on what was called Government Hill in 1876. Due to its configuration, the depot building was known as the Quadrangle. The garrison of the post moved to Government Hill in

1879, but the Headquarters, Department of Texas, stayed in town until 1881, when quarters were built west of the Quadrangle for the commanding general and his staff. This neighborhood was called the Lower Post, but it was eventually known as the Staff Post.

To accommodate the growing garrison in San Antonio, the War Department bought more land and started building permanent barracks and family quarters east of the Quadrangle. This was called the Upper Post, and, later, when its denizens included only infantry, it was called the Infantry Post. The Post at San Antonio grew to be the second-largest post in the nation. The new facilities and the presence of a well-developed community like San Antonio transformed service in Texas from a hardship to a very desirable assignment.

In 1890, the Post at San Antonio was at last given a proper name: Fort Sam Houston, in honor of Sam Houston—general, president of the Republic of Texas, governor of the State of Texas, and US senator from Texas. By 1892, Fort Sam Houston was considered "one of the heavens" toward which the eyes of the Army people turn. Garrison life included drill and ceremonies punctuated by dances and social events. There were trips to the firing range and occasional hikes and bivouacs in the surrounding countryside. The explosion of the battleship *Maine* in Havana Harbor brought a temporary end to the good life, as the garrison shipped out to Cuba, Puerto Rico, and the Philippines. Additional units were mobilized in San Antonio, including the 1st US Volunteer Cavalry—the Rough Riders. The United States acquired overseas territories to defend, and the Army was enlarged to accommodate this new mission. Fort Sam Houston was selected to house part of this increase, and more land was added to the post. This expansion made Fort Sam Houston the largest Army post.

The introduction of smokeless-powder small arms in 1892, the development of breech-loading field artillery, and the growth of San Antonio around and beyond the post rendered on-post target practice unsafe. The Army sought new training areas farther out of town. After temporarily leasing tracts of land for this purpose, the Army started buying land for a military reservation near León Springs in 1906.

Aviation was brought to Fort Sam Houston in 1910 when the Aviation Section of the Signal Corps, consisting of one airplane, arrived at the post. After Pancho Villa raided Columbus, New Mexico, a punitive expedition was dispatched into Mexico to pursue Villa. Along with it went the 1st Aero Squadron from Fort Sam Houston. In December 1916, Congress appropriated $13.2 million to develop San Antonio as "the Aviation base of the Army." Reconnaissances were made to identify an appropriate site. A location south of town was selected as the Aviation Post, South San Antonio.

In 1917, Fort Sam Houston was the largest Army post in the country, and its attention was focused on the border with Mexico. The declaration of war on April 6 changed that focus; the United States needed to quickly raise an expeditionary army of three million men with its attendant Air Service and send it overseas. The effect of this war on the military presence in San Antonio would be several orders of magnitude greater than during any previous or subsequent war. The number of troops that passed through Fort Sam Houston and Camp Travis, exclusive of those at the Air Service facilities, would exceed the total number of troops in the Army in 1916.

Army elements at Fort Sam Houston were concerned with several major endeavors. The headquarters of the Southern Department was responsible for mobilizing the troops in its four-state area for overseas service. A lesser concern was the security of the border with Mexico. Logistics was the bailiwick of the San Antonio General Depot. The depot supplied and supported the installations and units within the Southern Department. A major element was the Remount Depot, which provided horses to artillery, cavalry, and other units. Another element was a motor transport repair facility, Camp Normoyle, near Kelly Field. The garrison at the post rotated battalions and squadrons to the border area to maintain security there. The Army bought up the land between the main post and the Aviation Post and leased more than 3,000 acres to the east. Here they would build Camp Travis, a mobilization cantonment of more than 1,200 buildings, in three months. Camp Travis would organize and train two divisions, aggregating more than 20,000 men each.

In the spring of 1917, construction began at the aviation center of the Army with a recruit camp and a supply and maintenance facility. In the summer, a double-size flying field was started for the training of pilots. Designated as Kelly Field, these facilities were split into Kelly Field No. 1 and No. 2. Schools for mechanics and ground officers were established. Late in 1917, another flying field was established. Initially designated as Kelly Field No. 5, its earliest mission was the training of flight instructors. This field was designated as Brooks Field in December 1917. Brooks Field inaugurated a new system of pilot training called the Gosport System. Up to this time, student pilots had different instructors for each stage of training. In the Gosport System, the student pilot had the same instructor through all stages. In flight, the student was connected to the instructor by a voice tube so the instructor could give instructions and make corrections. In October 1918, this system was adopted for the whole Air Service.

The Leon Springs Military Reservation was 20 miles northwest of Fort Sam Houston. With the greatly expanded number of troops, more land was needed. Some 16,000 acres to the south were leased. The troops fired small arms and artillery and maneuvered there. An officer training camp and schools for cavalry and artillery were also established there.

When the doughboys came home from "over there," the Army went through its usual postwar contraction. Around the country, soldiers were out-processed and discharged while temporary mobilization facilities were closed. For the Army in San Antonio, there was a contraction of facilities, but there were also some significant additions. The San Antonio General Depot terminated the leases on several hundred thousand square feet of storage in the city as its workload decreased. But the amount of matériel to be managed was still significant. Construction of a new warehouse complex was completed northeast of the Quadrangle in 1922. Fort Sam Houston and the adjacent Camp Travis became the home of the 2nd Division. Fort Sam Houston absorbed Camp Travis in 1922 and maintained the title of largest Army post. The Leon Spring Military Reservation gave up its leased land, but the War Department acquired an additional 4,542 acres between 1920 and 1933, including the land on which the original Camp Bullis tent cantonment stood. This increase was needed to accommodate the 2nd Division and National Guard and Organized Reserve Corps units. Camp John Wise was closed, but the balloon school moved to Brooks Field. As the country settled into the Roaring Twenties, the stage was set for Military City, USA. San Antonio was host to four major military installations—its old friend Fort Sam Houston and three new ones, Brooks Field and the two Kelly Fields. Camp Bullis, Camp Stanley, Camp Normoyle, and the San Antonio Arsenal were also enlarged.

Although there were many more changes in the decades following the Great War, most involved the relocation of activities within the area or the absorption of facilities into existing ones. There would soon be Randolph Field, which assumed the flying training missions of Kelly and Brooks Fields. Kelly Field No. 1 was designated as Duncan Field in 1925, but it was absorbed by Kelly Field in 1943. Other changes occurred during World War II. Part of Kelly Field became the San Antonio Aviation Cadet Center, and it then became the separate Lackland Air Force Base and the "Gateway to the Air Force" in 1947, taking on the induction and training missions which originated in 1917 on Kelly Field No. 1. Camp Normoyle was also absorbed by Kelly Field in 1945 and became East Kelly Field. The San Antonio Arsenal began moving its ammunition storage and testing to Camp Stanley in 1920. The site was inactivated in 1947, and parts of the site itself were transferred to the city and the H.E. Butt grocery chain in 1972 and 1985, respectively.

The end of the Cold War saw a downsizing of military infrastructure. Kelly Air Force Base was closed in 2001. Its runway was transferred to Lackland Air Force Base to be used by the Air Force and the commercial tenants at the new Port San Antonio. The 24th Air Force Headquarters, three major and 16 other Air Force agencies, and several other federal agencies leased space at Port San Antonio. Contractors like Boeing perform maintenance on Air Force and commercial aircraft. Almost 60 other tenants work on the site. Rail facilities at the former East Kelly handle more than 5,000 railcars annually. Brooks Air Force Base was restructured in 2002, becoming Brooks City Base, with commercial and state and local government tenants. The transition was completed in 2011. Though the number of bases in San Antonio decreased, their influence on the nation remained. Randolph and Lackland Air Force Bases support the whole Air Force worldwide. Fort Sam Houston's tenants support medical training for all the services and conduct operations throughout the western hemisphere. The Installation Management Command and the Mission and Installation Contracting Command at Fort Sam Houston have worldwide responsibilities.

Today, many of the facilities used during World War I still exist. Although the prewar historical buildings at Fort Sam Houston still stand, Camp Travis is gone except for the street that bears that name. While troops still trudge along the dusty trails at Camp Bullis, they also move about by truck, helicopter, and C-130 transport. The San Antonio General Depot is long gone, as well as its 1922 warehouse complex. Kraus's Meat Market and the Signal Corps warehouse are still serving. Port San Antonio still has a few of its original buildings, and Brooks City Base has Hangar 9. Though the last American veteran of the Great War, Frank Buckles, died in 2011, several buildings in San Antonio that served during the war still stand, their service unknown by its citizenry. San Antonio retains its title as Military City, USA, by virtue of the growth during the "war to end all wars." The chapters that follow show the activities at each of the military installations in and around San Antonio and the lasting effects of that war.

One

"ONE OF THE HEAVENS"

In 1892, author Richard Harding Davis described Fort Sam Houston as "one of the heavens" toward which the eyes of the Army turned. Service there was desirable due to the quality of the facilities that had been built up on the post and the abundance of amenities in a town like San Antonio. Since 1845, the town and the post had grown up together, each benefiting from the other. Fort Sam Houston had become the largest Army post. By 1916, there was a major headquarters and an expanding supply depot in the Quadrangle, the oldest structure on the post. The staff of the headquarters lived in the adjacent Staff Post. The garrison was quartered in permanent buildings in separate neighborhoods for cavalry, infantry, and artillery. These troops trained at the Leon Springs Military Reservation, some 20 miles to the north. At the north end of Fort Sam Houston, the Aviation Post was established for the Air Service in 1914, along with the San Antonio Air Depot. Aero squadrons operated from here until the Remount Depot began to expand in 1916. The Air Depot then moved into San Antonio, and a new flying field was needed. With the Indian Wars becoming a distant memory, the Mexican border became the primary strategic focus. The Maneuver Camp of 1911 and the mobilization of the National Guard in response to Pancho Villa's raid on Columbus, New Mexico, in 1916 were the result of turmoil along the border.

The Alamo was one of the first facilities in San Antonio that the Army occupied. Army quartermasters put on a roof and used it as a supply depot. The top of the facade over the entrance doors was put there to conceal the gable end of the roof. The Long Barracks was occupied by the quartermaster's office and held medical, quartermaster, and ordnance stores. (FSHM.)

This view of San Antonio shows the area between East Houston Street (left) and Travis Park Church (right) in about 1890. The Vance Hotel can be seen to the left of the church. For most of the period between 1848 and 1861, the Army used the hotel as barracks for the Post at San Antonio (Courtesy of Martin Callahan.)

This view to the north shows Alamo Plaza, with the Alamo at the far right, in the heart of San Antonio around 1903. Since the Army first arrived in 1845, the city grew from 1,000 inhabitants to 53,000, making it the 71st-largest city in the country in 1903. By the end of the war, the population of San Antonio would triple. (FSHM.)

The Menger Hotel, next door to the Alamo, has been a landmark on Alamo Plaza since it was built in 1859. Seen here in 1910, the hotel has numbered Col. Robert E. Lee, Theodore Roosevelt, and Babe Ruth among its guests. Before becoming president, Lieutenant Colonel Roosevelt stayed here in 1898 while recruiting the Rough Riders. (FSHM.)

Three obsolete muzzle-loading cannons decorate the grounds of the San Antonio Arsenal in this early-20th-century postcard. Established in 1859, the arsenal was the only property in the city owned by the Army. By this time, the arsenal was repairing steel, breech-loading, rapid-fire cannons and magazine-fed small arms and storing ammunition. It remained here until 1920, when it moved to Camp Stanley. (FSHM.)

The 90-foot tower in the Quadrangle has come to symbolize Fort Sam Houston. Built to hold a 70,000-gallon water tank, the tank was replaced by a clock in 1882, when an alternate water supply was provided. The platform at the 60-foot level was a station for a watchman. (FSHM.)

Brig. Gen. Frank Wheaton (front row, center) and the staff of the Headquarters, Department of Texas, pose at Wheaton's quarters on the Lower Post in 1894. This department contained about a quarter of the Army. Standing at the far left is Medal of Honor recipient and future lieutenant general Arthur MacArthur. (FSHM.)

In 1894, completion of the Upper Post made Fort Sam Houston the second-largest post in the United States. Here, a 12-company garrison of all arms plus a band could be housed. There were 26 officer quarters and, for the first time, permanent quarters for married noncommissioned officers—four duplexes for the noncommissioned staff and one for the hospital steward. (FSHM.)

Firing at 600 yards.

Firers engage targets 600 yards away during Department of Texas rifle matches in 1888. This range, on land purchased in 1886 three miles from the post, was usable due to the sparsely populated land surrounding Fort Sam Houston. When San Antonio grew into the area north of the post and weapons became more powerful, the range could no longer be used. (FSHM.)

Lt. Col. Theodore Roosevelt (center) and two other Rough Riders of the 1st US Volunteer Cavalry sit on their mounts at Mission Concepcion, south of town. This outfit was mobilized in 1898 for service in Cuba. The regiment's campsite and training area was at the International Fair Grounds, about one mile to the northeast. (LOC.)

A hospital steward supervises litter drill in front of the post hospital. Regulations directed that the post surgeons supervise four hours of litter drill and first aid instruction for Hospital Corps privates each month. This 12-bed hospital was built in 1886 on the Lower Post. It would later serve as a dental clinic, a classroom, barracks, and, finally, a distinguished visitor quarters. (FSHM.)

Soldiers engage targets with their M1903 Springfield rifles at the new target range at Leon Springs. Due to the growth of San Antonio around Fort Sam Houston, it was no longer safe to fire small arms or artillery on the post. The Army bought up land about 20 miles north of the post for a military reservation. By 1917, this reservation totaled 17,274 acres. (FSHM.)

A field artillery section of M1902 field guns conducts service practice at the Leon Springs Military Reservation. Ammunition was in the caisson to the left of the gun. This gun was the first American cannon with a hydro-spring recoil system. With a range of 8,500 yards, it could not be safely fired at Fort Sam Houston. (FSHM.)

The officer of the guard, in front of the formation, inspects the rifle of a sentinel during a formal guard mount on the Infantry Post in about 1909. The guard detail members wear the full dress uniform and are armed with the M1903 rifle. The regimental band stands at the far left. (FSHM.)

The garrison of Fort Sam Houston, including the 26th Infantry Regiment, the 1st Cavalry Regiment, and the 2nd Battalion, Field Artillery, forms up on the parade ground on the Staff Post. The arrangement of the water tanks and the configuration of the clock in the tower date this George Bain photograph to between 1904 and 1907. (LOC.)

The Aviation Section poses with Signal Corps Aircraft No. 1. From left to right are (first row) Pfc. Felix Clarke, Sgt. Stephen J. Idzorek, Pfc. Bert Brown, Pfc. Vernon Burge, and Sgt. Herbert Marcuse; (second row) Oliver Simmons, Pfc. Bruce Pierce, Pvt. Glenn Madole, Pfc. Kenneth Kintzel, Pfc. Roy Hart, and William C. Abolin, cook. Not shown are master signal electrician Charles Chadburn, Pfc. Edward Eldard, and Pvt. Berkeley Hyde. (FSHM.)

15th Inf. encampment at Ft. Sam Houston, S. A. Tex.

The mobilization of the Maneuver Division at Fort Sam Houston in 1911 covered the cavalry drill ground with tents. Units were brought from all over the continental United States to try out the Army's new manual for tactical operations, the Field Service Regulations. The dark rectangular object on the skyline is one of the "aeroplane" hangars. (FSHM.)

The noncommissioned staff and band of the 18th Infantry pose in front of their tents at the 1911 Maneuver Camp. The staff noncommissioned officers are seated, with the bandsmen standing or on the ground. Seated from left to right are the bandmaster, a color sergeant, the regimental supply sergeant, two battalion sergeants major, and another color sergeant. (FSHM.)

Battalion Drill, Maneuver Grounds, Fort Sam Houston,
San Antonio, Texas.

Contrary to the caption on this postcard, this is not battalion drill. Rather, this is a parade by the entire Maneuver Division—some 12,000 infantry, cavalry, and field artillery, plus support troops. From March to July 1911, the Maneuver Division trained at Fort Sam Houston and at Leon Springs. (FSHM.)

An unidentified pilot of the 1st Aero Squadron stands in front of his Curtiss JN-3 aircraft on the cavalry drill ground after completing the squadron's 450-mile flight from Fort Sill, Oklahoma, to Fort Sam Houston on November 19, 1915. The squadron moved shortly afterward to the newly built Aviation Post, two miles to the northeast. (FSHM.)

At the north end of Fort Sam Houston, the Aviation Post took over the ground formerly used as a firing range and campground. Construction began in 1914 for an aero squadron. The two hangars to the right of the barracks provided shelter for 10 aircraft. The planes took off from the grassy field to the right. (FSHM.)

This L-shaped building at the Aviation Post was built for the aero squadron stationed there. Its four squad rooms and two NCO rooms accommodated 108 men. It also included an orderly room for the commander and first sergeant, a kitchen, a dining room, and a latrine. Nearby were the commanding officer's quarters and bachelor officer quarters. (FSHM.)

This 1916 aerial view of Fort Sam Houston shows the built-up portion of "the largest Army post." On the left beyond the chapel is the Infantry Post. The Cavalry and Light Artillery Post extends from the chapel to the right edge of the photograph, and beyond that are the Quadrangle and the Staff Post. The barn-like structure between the radio towers is the wireless station. (FSHM.)

When the National Guard was mobilized in 1916 during General Pershing's Punitive Expedition into Mexico, the tents of Camp Wilson stretched from the Gift Chapel, visible in the center skyline, to what was then the north end of the main post. Lt. Dwight D. Eisenhower was among the Regular Army officers training the guardsmen. (FSHM.)

INTERIOR OF
QUADRANGLE

Supply activities of the San Antonio General Depot have spilled out into the courtyard of the Quadrangle. During the mobilization of the National Guard in 1916, the volume of supplies needed to support the Southern Department and the National Guard units in the department quickly outstripped the capacity of the Quadrangle, requiring the leasing of storage and handling facilities in town. At the same time, the Southern Department Headquarters was expanding to

conduct a mobilization and to support the operations along the Mexican border. A temporary building was constructed in the courtyard (left of the tower) to provide more office space, but the solution would be to move all the supply activities out of the Quadrangle, leaving the headquarters as the sole occupant. (FSHM.)

Camp Cecil A. Lyon, shown here in 1916, was part of the Plattsburg camp movement. In this program, civilian volunteers, usually college students, underwent military training to become officers in the event of a national emergency. The trainees participated at their own expense and received no pay from the Army. The Plattsburg camps were a part of the preparedness movement and an

idea of former Army chief of staff Gen. Leonard Wood. General Wood believed that intelligent civilians could be turned into junior officers after a short period of intensive training. The camp was located northeast of the post chapel (visible on the skyline, left). (FSHM.)

Lt. and Mrs. Dwight D. Eisenhower stand on the steps of St. Louis College (now St. Mary's University) in San Antonio. Eisenhower, who had played football at the US Military Academy at West Point, was detailed by Maj. Gen. Frederick Funston, the Southern Department commander, to coach the St. Louis College team. (FSHM.)

Two of the 1st Aero Squadron's Curtiss JN-3 aircraft sit on the ground as the 1st Aero Squadron prepares to deploy to Mexico. Though the original caption on this postcard says that this is a scene at Kelly Field, both of these aircraft were destroyed in Mexico before Kelly Field was established. (FSHM.)

Two

SAN ANTONIO'S ARMY POST

There were three major activities at Fort Sam Houston during World War I: the Southern Department Headquarters, the San Antonio General Depot, and the garrison of the post. The principal operations of the department included patrolling the Mexican border, supervising the organization of units for overseas service, mobilization and mustering in of the National Guard of the states within the department, organization of US Guards battalions, and guarding utilities. In 1916, the department contained 41 Regular Army regiments. Of these, 17 would deploy overseas and another 7 were assigned to deploying divisions. The remaining 17 Regular Army regiments, mostly cavalry, patrolled the Mexican border. The department mobilized National Guard regiments and numerous smaller units from the states in the Southern Department. The six mobilization cantonments in the department received National Guard units and National Army draftees and formed them into eight divisions. The San Antonio General Depot managed the logistics for all of the above activities, including 45 posts, camps, stations, and airfields in the department. In 1916, the depot had 178,000 square feet of storage space. By November 1918, it had 654,000 square feet. In its warehouses on post and throughout the city, this depot received, stored, and issued quartermaster supplies, clothing, subsistence, meat, medical supplies, ordnance stores, and firewood while conducting salvage and reclamation activities. This depot also operated remount depots at Fort Sam Houston, the old Aviation Post, and Camp Stanley. The remount stations received and issued horses and mules at a rate of 1,000 per day. Their capacity was 17,000 horses and mules. Each of these animals consumed 24 pounds of forage daily, which was supplied by the depot. The garrison of Fort Sam Houston underwent the turmoil of mobilization as well. Units provided cadres of officers and noncommissioned officers for new units. The cavalry units rotated squadrons to the Mexican border area. The 3rd Field Artillery was assigned to the 6th Division and went overseas. The 19th Infantry was assigned to the 18th Division and moved to Camp Travis. It was preparing to go overseas when the war ended.

The Quadrangle at Fort Sam Houston housed the headquarters of the Southern Department, a regional command comprising the states of Texas, Oklahoma, New Mexico, and Arizona. In addition to guarding the Mexican border, the department was responsible for mobilization of the units of the National Guard and the National Army within those states. (FSHM.)

On the Infantry Post, the band barracks was converted to serve as an office for the new Chemical Warfare Service. This office was responsible for training in both the defense against and the employment of chemical weapons. These included toxic chemicals, such as poison gases, smoke, incendiaries, and flame weapons. (FSHM.)

An Army recruiting party sets up shop on Alamo Plaza in San Antonio. The recruiting officer (center) and his enlisted assistants are seeking volunteers to sign up for service. The soldier to the right of the recruiting officer wears the blue dress uniform. The others wear the olive drab service uniform. Behind them are the Gibbs Building (left) and the post office (right.) (FSHM.)

What U. S. Army is composed of.

This postcard, part of a portfolio of postcards illustrating Camp Travis in 1917, claims to show the ethnic diversity of the Army in the melting pot that is the United States. The uniforms these soldiers are wearing, however, indicate that the photograph was actually taken between 1902 and 1910. (FSHM.)

These barracks in the Cavalry Post were occupied by units of the 1st Cavalry Brigade during World War I. As no major role was envisioned for cavalry overseas, these units, the 3rd, 6th, and 14th Regiments, rotated from Fort Sam Houston to posts along the Rio Grande. Note the polo goals on the parade field. (FSHM.)

Members of the Telegraph Section of Company D, 51st Telegraph Battalion, stand on the steps of their barracks in the Cavalry Post. This unit shipped out to the port of embarkation in August 1918 and then to France. It returned to Fort Sam Houston in 1919 after occupation duty in Germany. (FSHM.)

The station hospital, built in 1908 with 84 beds and expanded to 152 beds in 1910, provided medical care to the garrison of Fort Sam Houston and supported the post hospitals of the smaller posts in the department. To support the increasing patient load, 19 temporary wards were built nearby during the mobilization in 1916. (FSHM.)

BROOKS FIELD AMBULANCE AIRPLANE - JN 4 D - LANDING ON PARADE GROUND, FORT SAM HOUSTON, TEXAS, SEPTEMBER 12, 1918.

On September 12, 1918, this modified Curtiss JN-4D hospital plane from Brooks Field landed on the Cavalry Post parade ground at Fort Sam Houston. Note the Medical Corps caduceus on the tail and the red cross on the fuselage. In the background are the cavalry barracks and the regimental headquarters building. (FSHM.)

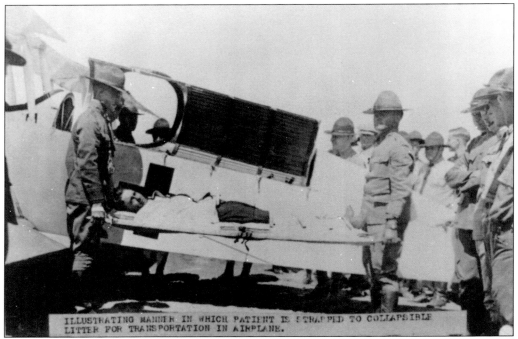

ILLUSTRATING MANNER IN WHICH PATIENT IS STRAPPED TO COLLAPSIBLE LITTER FOR TRANSPORTATION IN AIRPLANE.

Two medical officers carry a simulated patient in a demonstration of the Curtiss JN-4D hospital plane from Brooks Field on August 31, 1918, at Fort Sam Houston. Brig. Gen. James A. Ryan, the commanding officer of Fort Sam Houston, was one of the officers observing this early example of aeromedical evacuation. (FSHM.)

This aerial view, looking northeast, shows Fort Sam Houston in the foreground and the 15th National Army Cantonment, Camp Travis, in the distance. The Artillery Post is at the left, with the Quadrangle on the right. The 1,200 acres of land purchased for Camp Travis are covered with almost 1,300 temporary buildings. (FSHM.)

This view from the tower in the Quadrangle shows part of the Cavalry Post, the post chapel, and the adjacent civilian neighborhood. When the San Antonio General Depot needed to expand, the War Department purchased 293 acres east of the Quadrangle and began to clear this land for new warehouses. The only building not demolished was Kraus's Meat Market, pictured here with the Coca-Cola sign on its side. (FSHM.)

In this view, the neighborhood east of the Quadrangle has been cleared away. Kraus's Meat Market, now the meat branch of the retail store, can be seen at the far left edge of the image. Construction of the Signal Corps warehouse, which would be built in the open area to the right of the water tank, has not been started. (FSHM.)

Kraus's Meat Market, adapted to military use in 1917 to serve the American war effort, appears here in its military livery as the meat branch of the US Army Quartermaster Retail Store. Built before 1900, it is the only building at Fort Sam Houston with a civilian origin. (FSHM.)

The first building constructed in the new depot was a Signal Corps warehouse. The field telephones, wire, switchboards, buzzers, and signal flags used by the Signal Corps were stored at the warehouse. There, one would find all the paraphernalia required to support carrier pigeons on the battlefield. It was the only depot building completed before the armistice in 1918. (FSHM.)

The offices of the Warehousing Division of the San Antonio General Depot were located under the Hayes Street Bridge over the Galveston, Harrisburg & San Antonio Railroad tracks in San Antonio. The 600,000 square feet of warehouses leased by the depot were managed from these offices. Today, the Hayes Street Bridge has its own Facebook page. (FSHM.)

In 1918, the San Antonio General Depot leased this building and designated it as Warehouse No. 20. Built in 1905, it had been used by the San Antonio Machine & Supply Company until 1913. The depot used it for reclamation, a process in which worn and damaged equipment and clothing were stripped of usable materials for reuse. (FSHM.)

Warehouse No. 43, on South Flores Street across from the arsenal, was used for ordnance stores. This could include ammunition components and gun carriages but also cartridge belts, haversacks, canteens, mess kits, and saddles. It is one of the few leased facilities in the city not close to a rail line. (FSHM.)

The facilities of the San Antonio Macaroni Factory, on South Flores Street, were turned into Warehouse No. 39 for medical stores. These would include bandages, pharmaceuticals, medical kits, litters, medical instruments, and such. There were five medical supplies warehouses in San Antonio close to the Illinois & Great Northern Railway, including the Finck Cigar Factory. (FSHM.)

At the west end of the former Aviation Post stood this building, the headquarters for the 329th Auxiliary Remount Depot. This unit operated Remount Station No. 2, the Army's largest remount station. Remount depots were responsible for receiving, breaking, training, and issuing horses and mules for use by the animal-drawn units of the Army. (FSHM.)

Remount Depot No. 2 sprawled across more than 200 acres with its corrals, paddocks, and stables. There was a veterinary hospital and schools to train the blacksmiths, farriers, and packers needed to manage the horses and mules furnished by the remount depot. The remount depot also had its own rail siding and ramps to unload and load the animals. (FSHM.)

Maj. Reynold F. Migdalski, outfitted for a polo match, sits on his horse, Mosquito, on the Cavalry Post in 1918. A cavalryman and avid polo player, Major Migdalski was the commander of the 329th Auxiliary Remount Depot. These photographs of remount station activities were from an album maintained by Major Migdalski. (FSHM.)

Pvt. Selmar Jones shows off his riding skills. In civilian life, Private Jones had been a championship rodeo rider. As every day was a rodeo at the remount station, the Army recruited cowboys and assigned drafted cowboys to serve in the remount service, where their skills could be put to use. (FSHM.)

These two photographs illustrate a little-appreciated aspect of large-scale horse and mule propulsion. The remount depot, with 17,000 horses and mules, required not only the delivery of 221 tons of forage every day to feed the animals, but also the disposal of 128 tons of manure every day. The latter was achieved using the English packing method. The manure was placed in a compost heap 500 feet long, 100 feet wide, and 6 feet deep. It was piled in layers with straw in between. The heat of fermentation drove the fly larvae into the straw, which was removed periodically and burned. In 1918, Remount Depot No. 2 composted an estimated 40,000 tons of manure. (Both, FSHM.)

This 1918 panoramic view of Fort Sam Houston was taken from one of the radio towers on the Cavalry Post parade ground, looking southwest. At the left, the neighborhood east of the Quadrangle has been cleared away for the construction of a new general depot. Beyond the Quadrangle, the Staff Post, and the Artillery Post, the city of San Antonio has grown up around the post. The

military installation, which had been built more than two miles from the center of San Antonio, was now surrounded by the city, as San Antonio had grown from a population of 20,000 in 1876 to more than 150,000 in 1918. (FSHM.)

The general court-martial of 64 black soldiers for mutiny, murder, and other offenses takes place in the post chapel in November 1917. Following a series of racial incidents between the soldiers and the police in Houston in August, including an erroneous report that a soldier had been killed, more than 100 soldiers mutinied, taking their weapons into town seeking revenge upon the police. (FSHM.)

This sign marked the site where the executed mutineers were buried. A total of three courts-martial resulted from the Houston Riot in August 1917, with 19 defendants being sentenced to death by hanging and 91 being confined to terms from two years to life in prison. The execution was depicted in the 1979 television miniseries *Roots: The Next Generation*. (FSHM.)

Three

"The Mother of Armies"

Even though the contract for the construction of the camp was not awarded until June 22, 1917, representatives of the engineering firm Stone & Webster of Boston arrived in San Antonio to start work on the 15th National Army Cantonment on June 14 of that year. The cantonment would be named Camp Travis for Lt. Col. William B. Travis, defender of the Alamo. Stone & Webster employed a small army of workmen to build the camp. This army deployed with 77 saw outfits, 12 concrete mixers, nine trenching machines, three backfillers, 15 scrapers, five pumps, one car unloader, one steam shovel, five forges, and five plows. This equipment was supported by five water wagons, 60 three-ton trucks, 17 cars, three motorcycles, and four light trucks. The railroads brought in a total of 3,000 carloads of construction matériel, including 1,600 carloads of lumber, 15 carloads of nails, 160 of sewer pipe, 65 of other plumbing materials, 85 of water pipe, and 10 of assorted hardware. The maximum number of carloads received in a single day was 160, with 50 being the average number received each day. Construction of the 1,268 buildings of the camp consumed 35 million board-feet of lumber, 3,000 cubic yards of concrete, 125,000 pieces of hardware, 60,000 doors and windows, and 7,500 plumbing fixtures. In all, 25 miles of roads, 30 miles of sewer lines, 31 miles of water lines, and 12 miles of rail lines were built. The cantonment itself cost $6,717,176 to construct, and it could house 47,000 men. The buildings were models of Spartan simplicity, patterned after the standardized temporary buildings depicted in the *Quartermaster Manual of 1916*. Though construction at the camp continued through the war, the cantonment was essentially complete when the first Regular Army officers of the 90th Division cadre arrived on August 25, 1917, a mere 72 days after the start of construction. Here, the 90th Division, the 18th Division, and a host of smaller units were trained. A quarter of the divisions that served overseas received some troops from Camp Travis. After the war, Camp Travis demobilized more than 60,000 soldiers. The title of this chapter comes from E.B. Johns's 1919 book *Camp Travis and Its Part in the World War*.

A small army of workers shows up at the Camp Travis construction site. The contractor, Stone & Webster, employed a workforce of 7,000–9,100 people. On a typical day, there would be 8,645 workers, including 3,720 carpenters, 113 plumbers, 84 electricians, 237 teamsters, 455 office and field assistants, 3,616 laborers, and 420 Chinese workers. (FSHM.)

This standard two-story mobilization barracks accommodated 200 men. It was built using balloon-frame construction with double wood sheathing and composition roofing. In the one-story end was a kitchen with two ranges and a dining room that doubled as a classroom. There were 61 electric lights, 92 windows, and two heating stoves. (FSHM.)

Barracks were arranged in unit sets. That is, there were enough barracks and support buildings to accommodate the size unit to be billeted, whether an infantry or artillery regiment. The cantonment, in turn, consisted of sufficient numbers of unit sets to accommodate a whole division and its support units. Here, the latrine buildings, which housed showers, sinks, and toilets, can be seen between the barracks. (FSHM.)

Soldiers referred to this building near the south end of the camp as "the bull pen." Arriving recruits and draftees began their in-processing here with a physical examination and various tests to determine their skills. They would receive their uniforms and proceed to one of the units in the camp to begin their training. (FSHM.)

At the north end of the cantonment stood the facilities for the trench mortar battery, the quartermaster units, and the ordnance elements of the division. Rail lines, like the one in the foreground, threaded through the cantonment, facilitating the delivery of supplies. This photograph was taken from one of the fire station observation towers. (FSHM.)

The 90th Division's headquarters occupied this building at Camp Travis. The dial on the right wing of the building tracks the progress of the purchase of Liberty Loan bonds by division members. These bonds were one of the methods used by the government to raise money to prosecute the war. (FSHM.)

The laundry at Camp Travis could process two million pieces of laundry and 70,000 pieces of dry cleaning each month. It processed the laundry of Fort Sam Houston, Kelly Field, Brooks Field, and the other Army installations in San Antonio. The local newspapers credited the Camp Travis laundry as the largest in the world. (FSHM.)

Firemen from Fire Truck and Hose Company No. 315 pose with their engine at Fire Station No. 1. With almost 1,300 wooden buildings, Camp Travis needed robust firefighting capabilities. There were several observation towers and four fire stations distributed throughout the camp and Fort Sam Houston for this purpose. Most of the firemen were soldiers. (FSHM.)

This screened-in hospital ward was one of 38 wards in the hospital complex that served Camp Travis. This hospital complex included officer and nurse quarters, mess halls, laboratories, lavatories, a laundry, a chapel, and a mortuary. Staffed by 75 officers, 154 nurses, and 697 enlisted men, the Camp Travis hospital had a nominal capacity of 4,382 beds. (FSHM.)

This view to the south from one of the fire observation towers shows barracks as far as the eye can see. Camp Travis had a capacity of 47,000 soldiers and more than 3,500 horses and mules. The buildings included 241 barracks, 359 lavatories, 83 officer quarters, 22 guardhouses, 31 workshops, 17 post exchanges, 46 storehouses, a telephone exchange, a post office, and 280 stables. (FSHM.)

These two grain elevators at the south end of Camp Travis, where the rail lines entered the post, are 68 feet tall. They could hold 4,270,096 pounds of oats. This would equal the allowance for grain to feed the 17,000 horses and mules at the remount station for almost three weeks. The animals would also eat almost five million pounds of hay during that time. (FSHM.)

This building was the headquarters for Camp Travis's recreation programs. The War Department provided sports facilities, movie theaters, and libraries for the soldiers' entertainment. It also permitted religious groups and civic organizations to offer their services, including the Red Cross, the Knights of Columbus, the YMCA, the Salvation Army, the Jewish Welfare Board, the Masonic Welfare Office, and the American Library Association. (FSHM.)

THE EARLY BIRD CAPTURES THE STILL EMPTY CHAIR AT CAMP TRAVIS

At the Hostess House, like the one pictured here, the YMCA provided an appropriate environment for servicemen to meet and entertain visitors and family members. Advertisements for the Hostess House called it "a piece of Home." Julia Morgan of the YWCA developed the idea of the Hostess House (FSHM.)

At the south end of Camp Travis, a cluster of YMCA facilities, including an outdoor movie theater (lower left), supported troop morale. The open area behind the YMCA is the neighborhood cleared away for the new depot warehouse complex, and beyond that are the Signal Corps warehouse and the Infantry Post. (FSHM.)

The Liberty Theatre was one of the venues at which the War Department provided wholesome entertainment for mobilized soldiers. Built at a cost of $47,000 as the Majestic Camp Theatre, it opened on June 6, 1918. This 1,963-seat theater presented traveling shows, vaudeville, and motion pictures, including the feature in this photograph, *Friendly Enemies*. (FSHM.)

At YMCA No. 1, an officer from the YMCA (identified by his uniform and the insignia on his sleeve) conducts a bible study class for black soldiers in the 165th Depot Brigade at Camp Travis. The YMCA insisted that its services also be provided to black troops. The depot brigade in-processed the draftees and provided training or rehabilitation to bring them up to standard. (FSHM.)

Lined up for Mess.

A group of soldiers stands in line at their barracks waiting to go to lunch. They are carrying their mess kits. To provide cooks for the mass of troops at Camp Travis, the Army established a school for cooks and bakers at the camp in addition to the one at Fort Sam Houston. (FSHM.)

A dining room at Camp Travis stands ready to receive hungry troops. Dining room orderlies (DROs) served the troops by bringing platters of food to each table. Cafeteria-style feeding would not be instituted until just before World War II. The DROs and kitchen police (KPs), who helped the cooks, were detailed from the unit being fed. (FSHM.)

Maj. Gen. Henry T. Allen (front row, center) poses with the staff of the 90th Division at Camp Travis. General Allen, a cavalryman, was a veteran of the Spanish-American War, the Philippine Insurrection, and General Pershing's Punitive Expedition. Activation of this division began in August 1917, and it went overseas in May and June 1918. (FSHM.)

Groups of soldiers conduct dismounted drill in one of the many open areas provided within the cantonment for training. Dismounted drill was an essential building block of military discipline. It accustomed the men to respond to orders and to act as part of a unit. It also trained leaders to give orders. (FSHM.)

READING THE CAMP RULES.

Recruits gather around their officer for the reading of the camp rules. Army regulations required recruits to be instructed in the Articles of War, which prescribed the rules of discipline and soldierly behavior, including subordination to authority, absence without leave, and behavior before the enemy. The articles also prescribed the penalties for infractions. (FSHM.)

Making Wicker-work for Trench Sides.

Soldiers practice building gabions and other wicker items for use in the trenches. Gabions were used in the construction of field entrenchments, reinforcing the sides to prevent them from collapsing into the trench. Field expedients such as these were in use as early as the 15th century. (FSHM.)

56

As part of their training, these soldiers conduct "setting up" exercises. The object of these exercises was to develop the physical attributes of every soldier in terms of general health and vigor, muscular strength and endurance, self-reliance, smartness, activity, and precision, according to the Army's 1914 *Manual of Physical Training.* (FSHM.)

Recruits go for a run as their morning exercise. At the beginning of the 20th century, progressive thinkers in the Army began including physical training as part of the soldiers' training regimen. Calisthenics, setting up exercises, and long marches with full packs were included to increase the soldiers' strength and stamina. (FSHM.)

Bayonet Practice.

Doughboys engage the enemy, in the form of hay bales, with the bayonet. Skill with a bayonet was important in the close combat of clearing out trenches, where firing the rifle would endanger friendly troops. Bayonet training also fostered an aggressive fighting spirit. The blade of the bayonet seen here, the M1905, is 16 inches long. (FSHM.)

An officer from the 315th Engineer Regiment, 90th Division, oversees the construction of trenches and field fortifications near the barracks. Preparation and maintenance of trenches were essential skills "over there." Engineers also had to breach obstacles, such as wire entanglements, and build bridges. The 315th Engineers left Camp Travis for France in June 1918. (FSHM.)

These two photographs show soldiers from the 360th Infantry Regiment, 90th Division, turning out for training in their overcoats at an unusually snow-covered Camp Travis. The War Department had established 19 of the 30 cantonments for the National Guard and National Army in the South to take advantage of the better weather. But even in the "sunny south," snow was a possibility. In a typical winter, San Antonio would average less than one inch of snow per month. Capt. Gus Dittmar, a graduate of the First Officer Training Camp at Leon Springs, took these photographs. Dittmar would stay with the 90th Division until World War II. (Both, FSHM.)

A lone sentinel walks his post along D Street, one of the two main streets through the area occupied by the infantry brigades at Camp Travis. To reduce the number of soldiers detailed to guard duty stateside, the Army raised battalions of US Guards, which were composed of men not physically qualified for military service overseas but able to perform sentinel tasks. (FSHM.)

Soldiers of the 18th Division and their equipment assemble in the shape of the division's shoulder sleeve insignia. Called the Cactus Division, the 18th was the second division to be mobilized at Camp Travis, starting in August 1918. The war would end before the Cactus Division finished its training. (FSHM.)

Four

"Where America's Eagles Hatch"

The story of Kelly Field begins during General Pershing's Punitive Expedition. The Air Service was being expanded with San Antonio as the major aviation center, but the Aviation Post at Fort Sam Houston was deemed too small. Maj. Benjamin Foulois selected a site of about 700 acres near Leon Creek, five miles southwest of the city. In January 1917, the War Department took out a one-year lease for $11,924.26 for the site. Construction of hangars and other facilities began in March, and the 3rd Aero Squadron flew from Fort Sam Houston on May 5, 1917, and landed at the field, then dubbed Aviation Post, South San Antonio, Texas. This field was intended to be the largest and most important aviation training facility in the country. On June 11, the field was named Camp Kelly in honor of Lt. George E.M. Kelly, who was killed in a crash at Fort Sam Houston on May 10, 1911. It was renamed Kelly Field on July 30, 1917, and was soon expanded by another 1,800 acres. The original field (Kelly No. 1) became a recruit camp, and inductees flowed in for basic training. An Air Service Mechanics School was established there in March 1918 to train ground personnel for the burgeoning Air Service. To this was added a ground officers' school to train supply, engineering, and administrative officers to staff the squadrons and flying fields. The Aviation Supply Depot at Fort Sam Houston also moved to Kelly No. 1 in September 1917. The builder of Kelly Field No. 2 was Stone & Webster, who had also built Camp Travis. More than 100 buildings were erected, including 24 hangars, 12 barracks, and three large classroom buildings. The built-up area stretched a mile and a half. Kelly No. 2 could accommodate 500 flying students, up to 75 instructors, and more than 200 planes. By the end of the war, Kelly Fields No. 1 and No. 2 had graduated 1,459 pilots, 298 flight instructors, and more than 4,000 mechanics. They had also turned the flood of inductees into more than 500 squadrons for service at other installations. The title of this chapter paraphrases the caption in a cartoon from *Kelly Field in the Great World War*, by H.D. Kroll. The original caption was, "Where Uncle Sam's Eagles Hatch."

Soldiers from the 3rd Aero Squadron under the command of Capt. Thomas S. Bowen clear away brush, mesquite, and rattlesnakes from the land that would become Kelly Field. They also erected temporary buildings and guarded the site. On March 22, 1917, they began unloading hangars and aeroplanes. On the following day, they erected tent hangars for the aircraft. (AETC.)

Tent hangars, such as this one at Kelly Field, were developed to provide shelter for aircraft at temporary field locations. This one is in use as a machine shop for repairing aircraft. Note the field blacksmith's forge at the far right. Construction of standard steel hangars was begun on March 27, 1917. (AETC.)

Photo from an Aeroplane (handwritten on image)

This early view, probably in April 1917, of the Aviation Post in South San Antonio shows the field in operation. The large open area at the right served for takeoffs and landings. Tent hangars along two sides of the flying field accommodated the aircraft and maintenance operations. Tents for the Air Service personnel are at the left. (FSHM.)

Lt. George E.M. Kelly, in his dress uniform as an infantry officer, was killed in an aircraft crash at Fort Sam Houston in 1911. A native of London, England, and called Maurice by his fellow officers, Kelly enlisted in 1904. Camp Kelly was named in his honor on June 11, 1917, and renamed Kelly Field on July 30 of that year. (US Air Force photograph.)

Recruits for the Air Service line up at a mess tent at Kelly Field. The first recruits arrived on May 7, 1917. Within a week, the number of recruits at the camp exceeded 4,000. Here, the recruits were in-processed and put to work building the barracks and the water and sewer systems. (AETC.)

This aerial view shows the tent city at Camp Kelly in July 1917. Here, the Recruit Camp and Concentration Center received the recruits, organized them into 150-man squadrons, and shipped them to other installations. It served as the reception and replacement organization for the entire Air Service. (AETC.)

Rows upon rows of tents were home for hordes of recruits coming in to Camp Kelly. Some troops would spend up to a year living under canvas. Construction was limited to post exchanges, a telephone and telegraph building, a school, one barracks mess hall, a truck repair shop, an icehouse, two supply buildings, a root cellar, a bakery, and the commanding officer's quarters. (AETC.)

This aerial view shows the northeastern portion of Kelly Field No. 1. At the bottom are the two rail lines that served the camp. Frio City Road runs across the top. The primary flight school and the Enlisted Mechanics Training Department would initially be here. The Recruit Camp is located farther to the left on Frio City Road. (AETC.)

The Enlisted Mechanics Training Department, with its headquarters shown here, opened at Kelly Field No. 1 in October 1917. Here, mechanics and maintenance personnel were trained in the maintenance, repair, and rebuilding of aircraft. This school, with a capacity of 1,000 trainees, would produce more than 3,000 mechanics before the war ended. (FSHM.)

In the foreground is a row of sheet-metal buildings designed and built by Ernest Koerner. Although intended as hangars, they were converted to other uses, including instructional facilities for the Enlisted Mechanics Training Department. Their design resembles the two hangars that Koerner had built at the Aviation Post at Fort Sam Houston placed back-to-back. (AETC.)

This is one of the seven hangars used by the Enlisted Mechanics Training Department for training. Initially, the course was two weeks long, but it was gradually increased to three months, including an orientation flight. This served as a subtle reminder to the student mechanics of how crucial their work was. (FSHM.)

Established at the Aviation Post at Fort Sam Houston in 1914, the San Antonio Aviation Supply Depot operated briefly in San Antonio before starting to move to Kelly Field No. 1 in September 1917. The increase in flight operations led to this activity becoming an aviation general supply depot, expanding its facilities. (FSHM.)

In June 1918, construction was completed on this 300-foot-by-900-foot steel and concrete aviation supply warehouse on Kelly Field No. 1 for the San Antonio Aviation General Supply Depot. Internally divided into 11 separate warehouses, it received between 200 and 300 railcars of parts and matériel monthly. (AETC.)

The headquarters of the Flying Department at Kelly Field No. 2 operated the flying field, training officers, and aviation cadets for flying duty overseas. The device visible just to the left of the soldier walking by is a megaphone. It was used to amplify the bugle calls, which still regulated daily activities such as formations, meal times, and so forth. (FSHM.)

Driving along Frio City Road and passing through the left of these two gates would bring a visitor to Kelly Field No. 1. The right gate led to Kelly Field No. 2. These gates and the small white building can be seen to the right of the bungalow colony in the 1922 aerial photograph on page 107. (FSHM.)

The hangars at Kelly Field No. 2 were built to a standard plan designed by Albert Kahn. They featured wood framing and siding, asphalt shingle roofing, and a distinctive gambrel profile. Sliding doors were mounted on each end. The flight line ran along one side of the row of hangars. Other buildings necessary to support a flying field ran along the other side. (FSHM.)

Situated atop this hangar at Kelly Field No. 2 is a weather observation station. Knowledge of weather conditions was essential in conducting flight operations. Weather affected not only the direction of takeoffs and landings, but also the selection of routes, altitudes at which to operate, and whether operations should be conducted or canceled. (FSHM.)

Another type of standard hangar developed by the Air Service was the all-steel hangar, like this one at Kelly Field No. 2. Featuring a gambrel roof as well, these hangars were modular and could be built at varying lengths by adding modules. Hundreds of hangars of this type were built at Air Service fields around the country. (FSHM.)

Kelly Field No. 2 was designed as a "double unit" airfield with two standard-size flying fields placed end to end. This 1918 aerial photograph illustrates this plan. The two groups of 12 hangars comprising the two standard fields can be seen. The flight line is at the left. The open area beyond that is for takeoffs and landings. (AETC.)

Aviation cadets, identified by the white band on their campaign hats, arrive at Kelly Field for training. Their baggage and other gear are on the truck following them. During World War I, Kelly Field produced 1,666 aviation cadet graduates, the most from any of the Air Service's 25 flying training schools. (AETC.)

Aviation cadets report in to the Cadet Wing Headquarters at Kelly Field No. 2. Having completed ground school, these cadets were beginning a three-month course of instruction at the primary flight school, which, if completed successfully, would result in a rating of junior military aviator and a commission as an officer. (AETC.)

These aviation cadets undergo extensive instruction and rigorous testing at ground school, conducted inside a hangar. Completing ground school was the first step for aviation cadets on the road to becoming a pilot. Topics included aero engines, observation aviation, signaling, gunnery and bombing, aircraft construction, theories of flight, and meteorology. Ground school also included the traditional dose of dismounted drill and ceremonies. (AETC.)

This aircraft, a Curtiss JN-4 "Jenny," was the primary training aircraft for the Air Service. More than 6,000 models of this two-seat trainer were built by Curtiss, one Canadian manufacturer, and seven other US manufacturers. Most were powered by a 90-horsepower OX-5 engine. Thousands of American and Allied pilots learned to fly in this type machine. (FSHM.)

A student pilot and an instructor sit in a Jenny on the flight line of Kelly Field No. 2. When the Jenny was used as a trainer, the student-pilot sat in the front cockpit and the instructor in the rear. The instructor could observe the student during flight, but communication was difficult over the engine noise and the rush of air through the open cockpit. (AETC.)

An aviation cadet dons his flight gear in preparation for going aloft in a Jenny at Kelly Field. The leather coat protected the aviator from the wind and lower temperatures as altitude increased. The goggles protected his vision from not only the wind, but also the exhaust from the engine and the oil that leaked from the engine. (AETC.)

An instructor climbs into the rear cockpit of a Jenny at Kelly Field. A feature of the Gosport system of training, introduced at Brooks Field and adopted service-wide in 1918, was the use of a speaking tube, which allowed the instructor to talk to the student in the front cockpit over the noise of the engine. (AETC.)

The "meat wagon," a Ford ambulance, stands by at Kelly Field, just in case. Because crashes were frequent, the Air Service had fire equipment and medical support close at hand during flight operations. The Army Medical Department had developed a standard ambulance module that could be mounted on a number of different cargo truck chassis. (AETC.)

The ambulance crew prepares to deploy the stretcher as this meat wagon, a GMC model 16 converted into an ambulance, responds to the site of an accident. The aircraft to the right is a De Havilland DH-4. The casualty for whom the stretcher is intended is not visible. (AETC.)

Several Jenny trainers await their student pilots at Kelly Field No. 2. Other student pilots awaiting their turn in the cockpit sit under the shelter at the left. During their primary flight training, students received between 40 and 50 hours of flight time before taking their qualification tests. (US Air Force photograph.)

A De Havilland DH-4 with its engine running gets ready to take off. Based upon a battle-tested British design and built as an observation and day bombardment aircraft, the DH-4 was the only American-made aircraft to see service on the western front. A total of 4,846 DH-4s were built. (FSHM.)

A soldier prepares to climb into the gunner's station on a DH-4. The device mounted at this station is a Scarff ring. This device supported the weight of the two Lewis air-cooled machine guns (a total of 34 pounds) mounted there and allowed the gunner to elevate and traverse the guns over a broad field of fire. (AETC.)

Members of the 8th Aero Squadron conduct the manual of arms at Kelly Field during its early construction. While aviation cadets learned to fly, someone had to perform the more mundane tasks, including the provision of security at Kelly Field, which required a detail of 60 officers and men to staff the 23 guard posts. (AETC.)

This photograph motortruck and its trailer gave the Air Service a mobile laboratory and darkroom to process and print photographs in the field for tactical use. As the primary role of aircraft was observation, the Air Service made use of cameras to photograph the enemy's positions and activities. (AETC.)

The headquarters of Camp Normoyle occupied this building. The camp was home to the 304th Mechanical Repair Shop and the head office for District F of the Motor Transport Corps. This 88-acre site east of Kelly Field was established in May 1918 to conduct vehicle repair and motor transport operations. (FSHM.)

Camp Normoyle housed 32 barracks like this one. Construction of these facilities was authorized in June 1918 and continued through the end of the war. The enlisted men forming up in front of the barracks can be identified as mechanics by their fatigue uniforms and hats. (FSHM.)

The main repair shop at Camp Normoyle was the largest building on the installation. Measuring almost 500 feet by 500 feet, it covered more than five acres. In all, the American Construction Company completed approximately 70 buildings, a half mile of concrete road, and 4,830 linear feet of gravel road at this installation. (FSHM.)

This interior view of the main repair shop at Camp Normoyle shows the number and variety of tools and machinery on-site to repair and rebuild motor vehicles. The shafts with pulley wheels across the top of the shop are the power take-off systems to transfer power to the individual machines on the shop floor and work benches. (FSHM.)

Soldiers from the 145th Aero Squadron take a meal in their mess hall at Kelly Field No. 1. Meals were served family style—the platters of food were delivered to each table from the kitchen and passed around, each soldier taking a serving. The troops are wearing khaki cotton breeches and wool shirts. Standing in the back in white are the cooks. (AETC.)

Cooks pose with their mobile field kitchen at Kelly Field. This equipment carried all the necessities for cooking in the field. It was also used to provide meals at locations where mess halls had not been built. It was referred to as the "slum gun": slum from slumgullion, a type of stew, and gun from the chimney, which resembled a cannon barrel. (AETC.)

Soldiers gather at a mobile library truck at Kelly Field. The size of the two Kelly Fields, sprawling across some 2,500 acres, made it difficult for troops to get to the camp library. The solution was to send the library out on wheels to visit the troop areas. Note the military policeman at the far right. (LOC.)

This dayroom, or squadron recreation center, at Kelly Field provided the soldiers with a place to hang out during their off-duty time. This dayroom is equipped with a pool table, a piano, and a gramophone, as well as magazines, a reading table, and chairs for just sitting for a spell. (FSHM.)

A Curtiss JN-3 appears to fly over a column of trucks near some of the Kelly Field barracks. Like Signal Corps No. 42 and No. 52 on page 28, Signal Corps aircraft No. 48 was destroyed in Mexico long before Kelly Field was established. Photographers occasionally manipulated images to make them more interesting. (AETC.)

Five

AMERICA'S FOREMOST AIR SERVICE FLYING SCHOOL

Pleased at the prospect of the economic boost that the development of San Antonio as the aviation base of the Army would bring, the San Antonio Chamber of Commerce acquired an 873-acre tract southeast of the city near Berg's Mill and offered it as a site for a training field. The Army accepted the city's offer to lease the land when negotiations to purchase Stinson Field, home of the Stinson Flying School, failed. Thomas, Hardy & Company of St. Louis began construction on December 8, 1917. Rail lines were extended into the field and telephone lines were brought in. Thomas, Hardy & Company built 16 hangars along a curved flight line, six barracks (each with a mess hall), two 24-man officer quarters, an officers' mess, a hospital, a school, a post exchange, a YMCA, an administration building, a combination guardhouse and fire station, a supply building, an aero repair shop, a quartermaster supply building, a garage, a motor test facility, a machine shop, a blacksmith shop, a hose house, three gas buildings, a pump house, a water tower, and three buildings each for oil, gas, and water. And, of course, they constructed the flying field itself. Construction was completed in January 1918. Maj. Henry Conger Pratt was the first commander of this installation.

Originally called Kelly Field No. 5, it was designated as Brooks Field on February 4, 1918, in honor of Sidney J. Brooks, an aviation cadet. The initial mission of Brooks Field was to produce pilot instructors for other flying fields to teach aviation cadets how to fly. The Flying School Detachment had a capacity of 300 students. Total capacity at Brooks Field was 5,000 men. Officers at Brooks Field were directed to adapt the Gosport System, developed in England, for use at American flying fields. In October 1918, the War Department ordered the adoption of the Gosport System, as developed at Brooks Field, for all flying fields in the United States.

The headquarters of Brooks Field were located near the center of the curved flight line. It faced the hangar line and the open field used for takeoffs and landings. Behind it were all the administrative and support buildings necessary to operate the flying field. The firm Thomas, Harmon & Company built Brooks Field. (FSHM.)

Avn. Cadet Sidney J. Brooks Jr., a native of San Antonio, took his flight training at Kelly Field. Making his final qualification solo flight on November 13, 1917, he crashed on his approach to Kelly Field and was killed. He was commissioned and awarded his wings posthumously. Kelly Field No. 5 was renamed Brooks Field in his honor on February 4, 1918. (US Air Force photograph.)

Maj. Henry Conger Pratt, the "father of Brooks Field," stands by his Curtiss JN-4 aircraft. The insignia below the rear cockpit identifies this plane as one from Brooks Field. The cipher contains Pratt's initials, HCP, above his rating—JMA, for junior military aviator. The commander of Brooks Field, Major Pratt later commanded Kelly Field. (AETC.)

A formation of Air Service troops marches along the service road behind the hangar line. To their left front is the commanding officer's quarters. During the war, these quarters were occupied, in turn, by Maj. Henry Conger Pratt, Maj. Dean Smith, and Maj. Leo A. Walton. Beyond the commander's quarters is the post hospital. (FSHM.)

Near the eastern end of the hangar line was the aviation cadet training complex, with its barracks and classrooms. The initial mission of Brooks Field was the training of pilots. Soon, the training of pilot instructors was added. This six-week instructor's course had a capacity of 300 students. (AETC.)

This aerial view of Brooks Field, looking west, shows almost the entire extent of the construction. In the center foreground is the commanding officer's quarters. To its left, the line of 12 wooden hangars begins, with four steel hangars at the far end. On the flight line, 63 aircraft can be seen. (AETC.)

A Jenny has crashed onto the roof at Brooks Field. Here, a detail of soldiers is attempting to recover the aircraft. The light weight and low speed of the aircraft minimized the damage to the building. Nevertheless, flying was an inherently dangerous activity and fatal crashes were not infrequent. (US Air Force photograph.)

A sentry executes present arms at the entrance gate to Brooks Field. A sentry box has been built into the column behind him. The 1914 *Manual for Interior Guard Duty* prescribed the duties of sentinels in 12 general orders, which began, "I will take charge of this post and all Government property in view." (FSHM.)

This was the flying field for the carrier pigeons of Brooks Field. The Signal Corps was responsible for both of the Army's flying systems—airplanes and carrier pigeons. The pigeons could be carried by aircraft or ground troops and be released to deliver messages. The Army continued to use carrier pigeons during World War II. (FSHM.)

Brig. Gen. William A. "Billy" Mitchell conducts an inspection of Brooks Field in 1918. Mitchell is barely visible in the group passing the aircraft. He is partly concealed by the officer carrying the riding crop and is wearing a service cap. At the far left, in the short coat, stands the pilot of the plane being inspected. (US Air Force photograph.)

On November 30, 1918, an estimated 10,000 spectators came to Brooks Field to observe a "sham battle" in the area beyond the flight line. The demonstration included many of the features seen in France before the recent armistice: aerial combat, trenches, artillery firing, and gas attacks. The 18th Division at Fort Sam Houston provided the "American" troops; Brooks Field soldiers played the "Germans." (US Air Force photograph.)

A column of trucks halts at the entrance to Camp John Wise. This camp, about two and a half miles northwest of Fort Sam Houston, was established as an observation balloon training station in January 1918. Just inside the gate is the camp headquarters, identified by the presence of the flagpole. The camp commander marked this photograph as "censored and passed." (FSHM.)

Another view of Camp John Wise shows the tent camp and vehicle sheds with the troops standing by for the photographer. Beyond the tent area are two of the types of observation balloons used by artillery observers and a tent hangar. Each balloon required several support vehicles when deployed, including a winch vehicle to raise and lower the balloon. (FSHM.)

The commander and staff of Camp John Wise pose for a group picture in 1918. They are, from left to right, Lt. M.M. Turner, Lt. M.E. Franklin, Capt. F. Kehoe Jr., Lt. Col. D.H. Bower (commanding officer), Maj. A.H. Lambert, Capt. A.J. Lipsett, and Capt. J.K. Taylor. (FSHM.)

Six

"HELL'S FIRE AND FUZZIE-O"

In December 1916, the Leon Springs Military Reservation encompassed 17,274 acres. This had been adequate for a brigade-size garrison armed primarily with small arms and a limited amount of field artillery. The situation on the Mexican border brought an additional 12,000 troops to Camp Wilson—3,000 Regular Army troops and 9,000 from the National Guard. The amount of field artillery more than doubled. This required more acreage for firing ranges and training areas. When Fort Sam Houston was designated for a National Army Cantonment in May 1917, troop strength jumped by almost 50,000 men, while the amount of field artillery more than doubled again. To accommodate the increased number of troops, the Southern Department leased about 15,000 acres of land to the south of the existing military reservation. The reservation now extended beyond the town of Shavano to the intersection of the San Antonio & Aransas Pass Railway and Lockhill-Selma Road. As the National Army needed officers, the First Officer Training Camp was established in the northwest corner of the reservation, and it would turn out officers in three months' time—90-day wonders. Nearby, Camp Samuel F.B. Morse was established as a Signal Corps branch school where signal battalions and telegraph battalions were trained. Three other cantonments were built at Camp Stanley for the training of cavalry and field artillery. In July 1917, the 90th Division began rotating its infantry regiments to a tent camp near the Scheele Ranch. The 90th Division named this site Camp Bullis in honor of noted Indian fighter Brig. Gen. John Lapham Bullis. The engineer regiment of the 90th Division constructed the rifle and pistol ranges and other training facilities. The title of this chapter is from Gus Dittmar's book about his experience at the First Officer Training Camp. It recalls a chant muttered by Phillip Lingle, in the 2nd Company, First Officer Training Camp, trudging along the dusty trail to the Oppenheimer Ranch in the scorching heat, to keep himself going: "The bear jumped over the Panther Bluff/Hell's fire and Fuzzie-O." The chant was soon picked up by the entire company.

The building at the lower right was built in 1917 as the headquarters for the tent camp at the Leon Springs Military Reservation. It was built on part of the additional land leased to accommodate the increased number of troops being trained. The camp was designated as Camp Bullis in honor of John L. Bullis, 24th Infantry, the leader of the Seminole-Negro Scouts. (FSHM.)

The tent cantonment of Camp Bullis, shown here, was established on part of the leased land south of the original land acquisition. The 315th Engineer Regiment of the 90th Division constructed the camp. After marching or driving the 20 miles to Camp Bullis, units would remain in the tent camp while conducting field training and range firing. (FSHM.)

End of a Campt Street.—A Rifle Range.

Doughboys in training line up in the tent cantonment at Camp Bullis as they prepare to go to the nearby rifle ranges. After familiarization and mechanical training on their rifles, soldiers went through a 105-round practice qualification course at various ranges and firing positions, followed by a 60-round qualification course. (FSHM.)

Soldiers conduct target practice with their M1903 Springfield rifles. In addition to the ranges at Leon Springs, three more ranges were set up at Camp Travis, firing into the banks of Salado Creek. This allowed the troops to train within easy walking distance of the barracks rather than having to go 20 miles away to Camp Bullis. (FSHM.)

Temporary barracks, like these at Camp Stanley, were home for the troops of several training activities and a branch of the remount station. Three training camps for cavalry or field artillery and a cantonment for the US Guards were clustered with the First Officer Training Camp northwest of Camp Bullis. (FSHM.)

In the western part of the Leon Springs Military Reservation, a company of officer candidates march past their cantonment barracks at the First Officer Training Camp. Here, the "First Campers" underwent three months' training leading to a commission, hence the term "ninety day wonders." These training camps were needed to rapidly turn out the tens of thousands of junior officers needed for the expanding army. (FSHM.)

First Campers go to the rifle range at Camp Stanley. Along the firing line at the right, the shooters are in the prone position. The marksmanship training program also taught shooters to use the sitting, standing, and kneeling positions. The First Campers' barracks can be seen in the center background. (FSHM.)

Hundreds of First Campers participate in training near the rifle range at Camp Stanley, visible at the far left. As there were not enough firing positions, the troops received other types of training rather than waiting idly in line. This concurrent training could include field craft or other topics related to weapons firing. (FSHM.)

Here, the First Campers practice signaling using the semaphore system. The positions of the signaler's two hands indicate different letters of the alphabet or numbers. Use of flags made the positions of the hands more visible. Signalers could spell out words or use groups of letters to indicate phrases or tactical commands. (FSHM.)

This zigzag trench is being worked on by the First Campers. The rows of sandbags along the top edges of the trench prevent the edges from collapsing into the trench. The zigzagging reduced the effects of enemy fire from the flanks. This trench is far from complete by western front standards. It should be deeper, have fire steps and embrasures, and include dugouts for sleeping. (FSHM.)

Lt. Maury Maverick exemplified the kind of patriotic community leaders who attended the First Officer Training Camp. A lawyer before the war, Maverick served in the 1st Division in France and was awarded the Silver Star and the Purple Heart. After the war, he served in Congress and was elected mayor of San Antonio. (FSHM.)

A motorized machine gun company halts along the side of the road. Each of the divisions mobilized for the war had three machine gun companies to support the infantry, in addition to the machine gun units in the infantry regiments. One nonmotorized battalion supported each brigade. The motorized company supported the division as a whole. (FSHM.)

The New Machine Gun Companies, Carried on Fords.

After being mobilized at Camp Wilson, the 57th Infantry Regiment set up this camp at Camp Stanley in July 1917. The 57th Infantry had been formed from a cadre of officers and noncommissioned officers from the 19th Infantry at Fort Sam Houston. Included in this cadre was Lt. Dwight Eisenhower. (FSHM.)

Barbed-wire entanglements, such as this one at Leon Springs, were a major feature of combat on the western front. They were designed to hold attacking troops in place where they could be engaged by machine guns or artillery. Soldiers were trained in the building of such entanglements and in methods of defeating them, whether by blasting or manually cutting a path for the troops to pass through. (FSHM.)

A group of soldiers from the 410th Telegraph Battalion poses in front of their pup tents at Camp Samuel F.B. Morse, a sub-camp at Camp Stanley established as a school for Signal Corps troops. In addition to the 410th, two other Signal Corps battalions were stationed at this camp, and seven other Signal Corps battalions were created in the San Antonio area. (FSHM.)

Signalmen practice putting up communications wire, which would connect units by telegraph or field telephone. In rear areas where there was less danger of artillery fire cutting the line, the wire would be strung on trees or poles, as shown here. Near the front, the wire was usually buried. The soldier at the right wears a lineman's belt to assist in climbing poles. (FSHM.)

Troop K, 303rd Cavalry Regiment, pauses in its training for a group photograph at Camp Stanley. The 303rd Cavalry was one of the regiments organized at Camp Stanley. When the War Department determined that large amounts of cavalry were not needed, the 303rd Cavalry was transferred to Camp Travis. It was reorganized to form the 52nd and 53rd Field Artillery, both parts of the 18th Division. (FSHM.)

Artillery in Position—Ready to Fire.

According to the caption, this artillery battery is on position and ready to fire. These four guns are M1902 field guns of three-inch bore. Beside each of the guns is an ammunition caisson. As these are low-trajectory weapons and the trees at the right obstruct the line of fire, this battery is probably conducting service of the piece drills rather than live fire. (FSHM.)

Seven

"WHEN JOHNNY CAME MARCHING HOME"

World War I left San Antonio with a greatly increased military establishment. Not only had several new installations been added, but the sizes of the prewar installations had also increased. The city itself was 50 percent larger than it had been only 10 years before. With the armistice on November 11, 1918, demobilization began, and with it came a reduction of the amount of military activity, the closing of some installations, and the relocation of functions to the installations that remained in service. The soldiers of the partly mobilized 18th Division at Camp Travis were released, and the camp got a new occupant, the 2nd Division, in 1919. Camp Travis was then absorbed by Fort Sam Houston, which had grown from a prewar brigade post to a permanent division post. The San Antonio General Depot gave up its leased facilities in town and moved from the Quadrangle to a new warehouse complex. The headquarters of the Southern Department had grown, with additional responsibilities for mobilization, aviation, and chemical warfare. When reorganized in 1920 as the Eighth Corps Area, it retained those responsibilities and the staff to carry them out.

Camp John Wise closed, and balloon operations went to Brooks Field. More flight training was centralized in the San Antonio area, as Brooks Field became the Primary Flying School and Kelly Field No. 2 the Advanced Flying School. Kelly No. 1 got a new name, Duncan Field, and began to focus on logistics. Camp Normoyle was completed and became a permanent post. The Leon Springs Military Reservation gave up its leased land but added 4,543 acres by purchase and condemnation because the reservation had more people using it. Facilities and ranges were also improved.

More changes were in store for the military installations in San Antonio as they carried on through the Great Depression, World War II, the Cold War, and more. Nevertheless, San Antonio had become "Military City, USA," and it would continue to be so despite the changes.

Officers & Office Force Hdqrs Southern Department. Fort Sam Houston Texas. Feb. 18th 1919.

Members of the headquarters of the Southern Department assemble in the Quadrangle shortly after the end of the war. About a third of the staff can be seen in this excerpt from a panoramic photograph. When the headquarters first moved into the Quadrangle, the staff numbered only 14 officers and a few clerks. (FSHM.)

THE SECOND DIVISION, U.S.ARMY
BRIG.GEN. PAUL B. MALONE
COMMANDING
NOVEMBER 27, 1925   DESIGN LT. F.X. DORN
© G.F. Jennings.

In 1919, the 2nd Division returned from France and took up residence at the garrison at Fort Sam Houston. Units were billeted in Camp Travis, the Infantry Post, and the Artillery Post. Here, on November 27, 1925, the troops were turned out to be photographed and were arranged in the formation of their "Indianhead" shoulder sleeve insignia. (FSHM.)

The headquarters of the 2nd Division moved into the modified headquarters building (see page 52) at Camp Travis. The 2nd Division was the only division to be stationed at a single post. When the cantonment was being demolished, the headquarters moved into a building near the Gift Chapel. (FSHM.)

The barracks area of the Headquarters Troop of the 2nd Division at Camp Travis shows the return to peacetime soldiering. After the 2nd Division took up residence at Fort Sam Houston in 1919, area beautification, such as this display, resumed to fill the troops' idle hours after World War I. (FSHM.)

Upon their return from overseas, elements of the 15th Field Artillery Regiment were billeted in these Camp Travis barracks. Though only two years old, these temporary barracks are already becoming quite ramshackle in this photograph. They were drafty, they leaked, and they were a fire hazard. The mobilization barracks at all of the San Antonio military installations were in similar condition. (FSHM.)

Temporary barracks converted into apartments also became ramshackle very quickly, such as the ones seen here in 1923. The living conditions for the Army all across the country prompted the passage of the Army Housing Act of 1926 by Congress. The temporaries were replaced by well-designed permanent facilities as a means of retaining veterans and recruits. (FSHM.)

The Aviation Post at Fort Sam Houston resumed flight operations in 1925, as the remount station was phased out. The 12th Observation Squadron operated from this field in support of the 2nd Division. In 1928, it was designated as Dodd Field in honor of pioneer aviator Col. Townsend F. Dodd. (FSHM.)

Lt. Clarence Edge stands next to a Consolidated O-17 at Dodd Field. Lieutenant Edge and a detachment of five members of the Coast Guard flew from Dodd Field, starting in 1934, to support customs enforcement against smugglers along the Mexican border. The US Coast Guard was the last aviation organization to operate out of Dodd Field. (FSHM.)

These 38 warehouses at the San Antonio General Depot were completed in 1921 to replace the rented space in San Antonio. Each of these corrugated-iron buildings measured 80 feet by 200 feet and had concrete floors and loading docks. They could be accessed by both trains and trucks. The complex cost $1,666,015 to build. (FSHM.)

Members of the Air Service at Kelly Field assemble for a group photograph in the shape of an airplane in 1919. This follows the wartime tradition for unit photographs, usually in the shape of the unit shoulder sleeve insignia (see page 60). Kelly Field had no shoulder sleeve insignia, but the airplane was an appropriate symbol to represent this premier flying field. (FSHM.)

This 1922 aerial view of Kelly Field shows Kelly No. 1 to the left of the road. Depot facilities are in the foreground, with the Recruit Brigade in the distance. In the near foreground is a cluster of seven bungalows that were built to alleviate the shortage of permanent party officer quarters. Part of Kelly No. 2 can be seen at the far right. (AETC.)

This low-level image captures part of the west end of the Kelly No. 2 flight line. At this time, all flight training, including the Advanced Flying School, was centralized at Kelly Field. In 1920, the Air Service became the Air Corps, a separate branch of the Regular Army. (FSHM.)

An SE-5 scout plane prepares to take off at Kelly Field. The Air Service acquired 95 of the British-designed SE-5s in 1918. On the side of the fuselage is the insignia of the 95th Aero Squadron. This unit continues in service today at Offutt Air Force Base as the 95th Reconnaissance Squadron. (FSHM.)

An SE-5 gets ready to take off at Kelly Field. After the war, these aircraft were used as advanced trainers. Designed to be easy to fly, the SE-5 had a top speed of 138 miles per hour. The Air Service resumed using the white star in a blue circle insignia on its aircraft in 1920. (FSHM.)

A soldier stands at the main gate of the now permanent Camp Normoyle. The camp was designated as a motor transport general depot. It continued to procure and store motor vehicle supplies and repair motor vehicles. The Works Progress Administration constructed the entrance during the Great Depression. (FSHM.)

In the 1920s, Camp Normoyle's motor repair shops were also used for a motor repair school and an Army vocational school. During World War II, Camp Normoyle served as a quartermaster, ordnance, and engineer depot for Kelly Field. In 1944, Camp Normoyle was merged with Kelly Field and was referred to as East Kelly. (FSHM.)

This aerial view of Brooks Field in 1926 shows the base at the midpoint of its role as the Primary Flying School. Parked along the flight line are 80 planes, with another six vacant parking slots. For the next five years, Brooks Field would also be the home of the School of Aviation Medicine. (US Air Force photograph.)

Airship C-2 hovers near the balloon hangar at Brooks Field. This 1,000-foot-long balloon hangar was built in 1919. The airship program was short-lived. After airship C-2 exploded on takeoff on October 2, 1922, at Brooks Field, the Army began to reconsider the usefulness of the airship program. Only the huge hangar remained as evidence of these operations. (US Air Force photograph.)

In 1928 and 1929, the Air Corps conducted a series of experiments involving the delivery of military forces to the battlefield by parachute. In this photograph, soldiers prepare to "hit the silk" from a De Havilland DH-4. Besides the two paratroopers on the wings, it looks like a third is diving off the right side of the plane behind the wing. (US Air Force photograph.)

This color postcard shows a multi-plane drop over Brooks Field. An official demonstration on September 29, 1929, saw a platoon-size force of 18 men descend on Brooks Field. Their Lewis machine guns were dropped in padded containers. In 1940 and 1941, these tests would lead to additional tests and exercises at Fort Sam Houston, with Air Corps transports and gliders ferrying 2nd Division troops to maneuvers near Brackettville, Texas, and in North Carolina. (US Air Force photograph.)

Curtiss JN-4 aircraft are lined up for inspection near Hangar No. 9 at Brooks Field in 1920. The flags mounted on the car at the lower left indicate that the inspecting officer is a general officer. At this time, Brooks Field was in the process of becoming the home of the Balloon and Airship School. (US Air Force photograph.)

Civilian spectators watch as six aircraft take off from Brooks Field during the filming of the motion picture *Wings*. This classic war film by William Wellman and Paramount Pictures, which received the first Academy Award for Best Picture, was filmed at Fort Sam Houston, Kelly Field, and Camp Stanley. (US Air Force photograph.)

During the climactic recreation of the Battle of Saint-Mihiel in *Wings*, American aircraft conduct a low-level attack as the infantry and tanks advance. This action took place along the eastern side of Camp Stanley, with the American and German troops played by the 2nd Division from Fort Sam Houston. (FSHM.)

The cause of the demise of the San Antonio Arsenal's ammunition storage function can be seen in this 1921 aerial photograph. As the arsenal was completely surrounded by San Antonio, it was inadvisable to have tons of munitions inside the city. In 1920, the ammunition was moved to Camp Stanley. In 1933, the Camp Stanley ammunition storage area was transferred to the Ordnance Department. (FSHM.)

To better support the year-round cycle of training at Camp Bullis, this cantonment, east of the original camp headquarters, was started in 1930. Mobilization-type mess halls and latrines with flush toilets were built at opposite ends of long rows of tent frames. An administration building, post exchange, hostess house, infirmary, and general officer house were also added. (FSHM.)

Battery B, 4th Field Artillery, a pack or mountain artillery unit, occupies a position at Camp Stanley with its howitzers. When the 4th Field Artillery was transferred to the Panama Canal Zone in 1922, it was the last unit to be stationed at Camp Stanley. The camp then functioned as an ammunition storage facility. (FSHM.)

Eight

WHERE ARE THEY NOW?

Despite the passage of almost 100 years since the end of "the war to end all wars," many of the buildings that served a military purpose during World War I are still standing, even quite a few that were not on military bases. More than 200 of the prewar buildings at Fort Sam Houston are included in its National Historic Landmark District. Of the wartime construction at Fort Sam Houston, all of Camp Travis is gone, with most of its temporary buildings coming down in 1928. The last Camp Travis building, the brick portion of the laundry, was demolished in 2006. Only one permanent building constructed during wartime remains in the depot area. Kelly Field and Brooks Field were closed in the various Base Realignment and Closure Acts, with most of their functions transferred to Lackland and Randolph Air Force Bases. Yet, a few of their World War I buildings survive. Port San Antonio carries on some of Kelly Field's logistic functions and still has an Air Force presence.

The San Antonio Arsenal transferred all of its ammunition-related functions to Camp Stanley after the war and was deactivated in 1947. The arsenal was converted to other government purposes, including the Naval Reserve. Part of the property was transferred to the city in 1972 for a park. The remainder was sold by the Department of Defense to the H.E. Butt grocery chain (HEB) in 1985, and several of its prewar buildings are in use as HEB's corporate headquarters. Camp Stanley was transferred to the Ordnance Department in 1933. Of the buildings leased by the War Department in San Antonio, quite a few still stand, although they have been repurposed. Camouflage-clad men and women still trudge the hot, dusty trails at Camp Bullis, as they did when "Hell's Fire and Fuzzie-O" propelled the 2nd Company on to its objective. In 1917, all the bases were under the command of the Southern Department, with its headquarters in the Quadrangle. Today, all the military installations are part of Joint Base San Antonio, with its headquarters a stone's throw from that same Quadrangle.

This sign greets visitors to Fort Sam Houston. In 2009, Joint Base San Antonio was established, combining Fort Sam Houston, Randolph Air Force Base, and Lackland Air Force Base into the largest joint base in the country. An Air Force element, the 502nd Air Base Wing, commands Joint Base San Antonio from its headquarters at Fort Sam Houston. (Courtesy of Martin Callahan.)

Lt. Gen. Guy Swann III and the people of the Headquarters, US Army North, stand before the clock tower in the Quadrangle on May 6, 2011. Army North is responsible for the land defense of the United States and civil support operations. The author of this book can be seen standing in the middle behind the group of four soldiers kneeling at the lower right. (US Army photograph.)

The Long Barracks was renovated in 2012 as a home for the Mission and Installation Contracting Command. Home to the 23rd Infantry after World War I, a reception center during the Korean War, and basic training barracks for conscientious objector medics in the Vietnam War, it had been vacant for two decades due to structural problems. (Photograph by the author.)

This brick part of the laundry, the last remaining Camp Travis building at Fort Sam Houston, was demolished in 2006. Laundry service had been discontinued in January 1999. This site is planned to be part of Freedom's Crossing, a community center including shops, eateries, a commissary, a post exchange, and a hotel. (FSHM.)

The only vestige of Camp Travis at Fort Sam Houston is Camp Travis Road, which runs past the post exchange service station and shoppette. This area is near the southernmost part of the camp's location. In 2002, Fort Sam Houston renamed a service road to commemorate this long-gone National Army cantonment. (Photograph by the author.)

Not far from the original main gate to the two Kelly Fields stands this new sign for Port San Antonio. Just to the left is the bungalow colony. Ahead are the Air Force enclave and the old flight line. They have kept the name Kelly Field for this portion of the installation. (Photograph by the author.)

Aviation giants Boeing and Lockheed Martin now work out of some of the maintenance facilities formerly used by the San Antonio Air Logistics Center at Kelly Air Force Base. General Dynamics also works not far from here at Port San Antonio. These companies work on civil aircraft in addition to their military contracts. (Photograph by the author.)

In the words of Col. Henry Conger Pratt, commander of Kelly Field, the bungalow colony was built at Kelly Field because "accommodations are as bad as at any field in the country." As the oldest collection of Air Service family quarters, the bungalow colony was listed in the National Register of Historic Places in 2003. (Photograph by the author.)

This bungalow began life as an infirmary in 1918. Converted to officer quarters in 1920, it was converted into an officers' club in 1941 and a guest house in 1943. In 1964, it was used as general officer quarters. From 1969 until Kelly Air Force Base closed, it was the home of the vice commander of the San Antonio Air Logistics Center. (Photograph by the author.)

This "Brooks City-Base" sign stands not far from where the curved flight line of Brooks Field ended. This converted installation comprises more than 1,000 acres of real estate for mixed-use development. Tenant activities include health care, pharmaceuticals, bioscience, biomedicine, education, information technology, and alternative energy. There are also residential developments as well as eateries and supermarkets on-site. (Photograph by the author).

Hangar 9 at Brooks City Base is not only the sole remaining building at that location built during World War I, it is also the oldest wooden Air Force hangar. Although it served as the US Air Force Museum of Aerospace Medicine, its future hangs in the balance as of this writing. (Photograph by the author.)

Edmond J. Felt, a San Antonian who trained as a balloonist at Camp John Wise during the war, points at the marker commemorating the camp and balloon school in 1971. The site of the camp, about a mile south of the marker, is now a quiet suburban neighborhood in the Olmos Basin. (FSHM.)

The building that once housed Kraus's Meat Market is now used by the 502nd Security Forces Squadron, part of the mission support group that operates the post. Officers of the Air Force Police now man the access control points and provide internal security for this joint base (see page 36). (Photograph by the author.)

The Signal Corps warehouse continued in that role through World War II. During that war, the guards at the San Antonio General Depot conducted target practice in the basement. Since then, the building has been used by the Fourth Army Map Depot, the Army Map Service, and the Defense Mapping Agency. It now provides office space for the Army Medical Department Center and School. (Photograph by the author.)

This former reclamation warehouse is now the 13th Floor Haunted House (see page 37 for its wartime appearance). It is billed as the largest haunted attraction in San Antonio. After World War I, it briefly served as a hotel for railroad passengers traveling at the Sunset station, which is located across the street. In addition to tours and Halloween parties, it currently offers a three-story thrill slide. (Photograph by the author.)

The former Warehouse No. 39, a medical supply facility at 1906 South Flores Street, is now the 1906 Complex, established in 1991 as a design studio, custom frame shop, and gallery. It is now an anchor for the San Antonio art community (see page 38 for its wartime appearance). (Photograph by the author.)

After World War I, the former Warehouse No. 43 was owned by the A.I. Root Candle Company of Medina, Ohio, and then the H.E. Butt grocery store chain, which has had its corporate headquarters across the street since 1985 (see page 38 for its wartime appearance). (Photograph by the author.)

After almost 100 years, the headquarters for Camp Bullis is still in the same building, though the building has been considerably modified. Trainees from the Medical Education and Training Campus at Fort Sam Houston are the main customers, followed by Air Force Security Police trainees, the Army Reserve, and the National Guard. (Photograph by the author.)

Soldiers move through the fully instrumented urban warfare complex at Camp Bullis. In addition to maneuver areas and modern firing ranges, the camp has a forward operating base, a drop zone, and a combat assault landing strip. The Air Force Security Police conduct convoy security training here and use state-of-the-art simulators for part of the training. (US Army photograph.)

The commanding officer quarters and a few of the storage buildings in use during the war still stand at the San Antonio Arsenal. In 1972, part of the site was transferred to the City of San Antonio. This became the Commander's House Adult and Senior Citizens Center. Since 1985, the arsenal has served as the corporate headquarters of the H.E. Butt chain of grocery stores. (HABS photograph.)

On the grounds of the former San Antonio Arsenal, this storehouse, built in 1883, was another one of the buildings acquired by the H.E. Butt chain of grocery stores. Although the San Antonio Arsenal had closed in 1947, the property was still used by the federal government, including the Navy Reserve. (Photograph by the author.)

The headquarters of the 502nd Airbase Wing occupied this building at Fort Sam Houston in 2011. Built between two historic neighborhoods, it bears design elements from the Quadrangle and the Cavalry Post. The Air Service consisted of one plane and a handful of men 104 years ago. Today, an Air Force general commands the largest joint base in the country from this building. (FSHM.)

About Preservation
Fort Sam Houston

Preservation Fort Sam Houston, Inc., a 501(c)(3) private nonprofit educational organization not affiliated with the Department of Defense, was established in 1984 to serve as an advocate for historic preservation at Fort Sam Houston and to support the activities of the Fort Sam Houston Museum. The organization participates with Fort Sam Houston in the preservation process as an interested party in the local community. It has pioneered the concept of the public-profit partnership for preservation projects on military installations. After obtaining an out-grant from the Army for the use of the dilapidated Stilwell House, the organization carried out a series of fundraising programs to renovate the building. The Army funded the required lead and asbestos abatement and installed a new standing-seam metal roof. By 1998, the Stilwell House had been restored to its previous grandeur. Preservation Fort Sam Houston held a grand reopening of the Stilwell House as a dual-use community facility that is available to military organizations at Fort Sam Houston for meetings and other official functions. It also serves as the organization's headquarters and a venue for its meetings and special events. In 2013, the organization nominated Fort Sam Houston for a Richard H. Driehaus Preservation Award from the National Trust for Historic Preservation, recognizing Fort Sam Houston for its partnership in federal preservation. The award was presented on November 1, 2013. Preservation Fort Sam Houston has continued its efforts to promote historic preservation and its support of the Fort Sam Houston Museum.

DISCOVER THOUSANDS OF LOCAL HISTORY BOOKS
FEATURING MILLIONS OF VINTAGE IMAGES

Arcadia Publishing, the leading local history publisher in the United States, is committed to making history accessible and meaningful through publishing books that celebrate and preserve the heritage of America's people and places.

Find more books like this at
www.arcadiapublishing.com

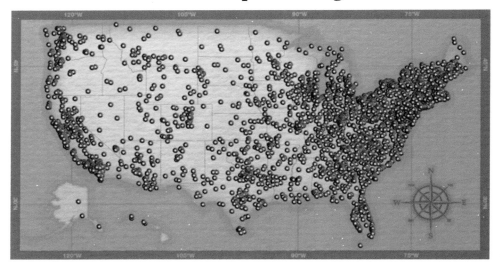

Search for your hometown history, your old stomping grounds, and even your favorite sports team.

Consistent with our mission to preserve history on a local level, this book was printed in South Carolina on American-made paper and manufactured entirely in the United States. Products carrying the accredited Forest Stewardship Council (FSC) label are printed on 100 percent FSC-certified paper.

MADE IN THE